Y0-DXI-677

MADELINE'S RESCUE

by
Ludwig Bemelmans

Teacher Guide

Written by
Jean Jamieson

Note

The Scholastic paperback edition of the book was used to prepare this teacher guide. The page references may differ in the hardcover or other paperback editions.

ISBN 1-56137-473-3

To order, contact your local
school supply store, or—

Novel Units, Inc.
P.O. Box 791610
San Antonio, TX 78279

Table of Contents

Skills and Strategies

Thinking
Brainstorming

Writing
Creative writing,
letter writing

Listening/Speaking
Discussion, guest speaker

Comprehension
Predicting, comparison/
contrast

Literary Elements
Poetry

Other
Graphic, metric system,
recipes, music, geography

Summary of *Madeline's Rescue*

The smallest of twelve girls living with Miss Clavel in a house in Paris, Madeline slips and falls off of the bridge as they are taking a walk together. Rescued from a watery grave by a dog, Madeline and the other girls take the dog back to the house.

Months later, troubles descend upon them when the trustees make the annual inspection and declare that the dog, now named Genevieve, must go. The story relates the resultant search for Genevieve, her arrival back at the home, and the resolution of the problem faced by Miss Clavel, as all of the girls declare "Genevieve is mine tonight."

About the Author/Illustrator

Ludwig Bemelmans was born April 27, 1898, in Meran, Tirol, Austria, now part of Italy. He attended public and private schools in Austria before dropping out at the age of sixteen. He came to the United States in 1914, and was naturalized in 1918. He married Madeline Freund in 1935, and they had one daughter, Barbara. He died October 1, 1962, and is buried in Arlington, Virginia.

Bemelmans was a writer, humorist, illustrator, painter, and author of books for children. He worked in hotels and restaurants from 1914-17, and after World War I he became a waiter and later part owner of Hapsburg House in New York. He won the Caldecott Medal in 1953 for *Madeline's Rescue*.

About the character Madeline he said, "I have repeatedly said two things that no one takes seriously, and they are that first of all I am not a writer but a painter, and secondly that I have no imagination. It is very curious that, with my lack of these important essentials, the character of Madeline came to be. It accounts perhaps for her strength; she insisted on being born. Before she came into the world, I painted. That is I placed canvas or paper on an easel before me and made pictures. I found in this complete happiness and satisfaction."

"You will notice in *Madeline* that there is very little text and there is a lot of pictures. The text allows me the most varied type of illustration."

"Her beginnings can be traced to stories my mother told me of her life as a little girl in the convent of Aloetting in Bavaria. I visited this convent with her and saw the little beds in straight rows, and the long table with the washbasins at which the girls had brushed their teeth."

"In the sequel, (*Madeline's Rescue*), Madeline shares the pages with a dog. This dog came about in a strange way. Two neighbor girls requested another *Madeline* story. I offered them fifty cents apiece if they would give me an idea, for I was paralyzed with lack of imagination."

The plot that the girls came up with, "Madeline has a dog, and the dog is taken away but it comes back again, maybe with puppies so all the girls can have dogs," was the beginning of a new story.

Bemelmans is quoted as having said, "The portrait of life is the most important work of the artist and it is good only when you've seen it, when you've touched it, when you know it. Then you can breathe life onto canvas and paper."

The Caldecott Medal

The Caldecott Medal, named for Randolph Caldecott, is awarded annually by the American Library Association to the illustrator of the most distinguished American Picture Book for Children. The medal was awarded to Ludwig Bemelmans for *Madeline's Rescue* in 1954.

Randolph Caldecott, an English illustrator, was born in Chester, England, March 22, 1846. He died in St. Augustine, Florida, February 12, 1886. He had a great talent, and loved horses, dogs, and everything that belonged to the English countryside. His drawings were noted for their freshness boldness, and gaiety. He thought long and seriously before putting pen to paper. He said, "The fewer the lines, the less error committed!"

Although Caldecott and his wife never had children of their own, he had many children as friends. It was for children that he did the work for which he will probably be longest remembered, and best loved.

Introductory Activities

You may choose to do one of these activities before reading the story, and the other activities after reading the story. They are appropriate at any time.

1. France: Make some banners that have words in the French language on them, and hang them in the room. (You may wish to make them red, white, and blue, to go with the colors of the bulletin board. See Bulletin Board Ideas, France. See Teacher Information section for a listing of some words in French.)

   Have a record or a tape of a French recording artist playing when the children arrive. (See Audio-Visual Bibliography.)

   After the children gather in a group, ask them to look at the bulletin board. Brainstorm with them as to what that might represent. Accept all ideas, and list them as they are given.

   Tell the children that the bulletin board is a representation of the flag of France. Compare the flag of France to the flag of your country. Are they alike in any way? How are they different? Use a Venn Diagram to record the comparisons.

French Flag   U.S. Flag

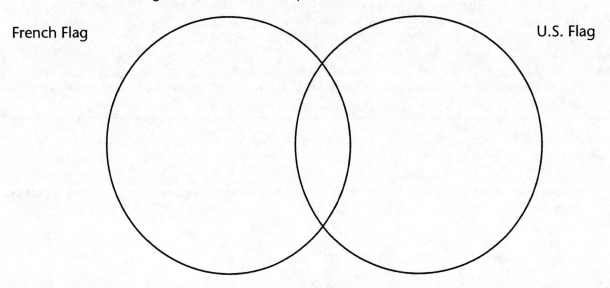

2. Pets: Make a copy of a poem about a pet and have it in the area where the children will gather. (See Bibliography/dePaola and Prelutsky.)

   After the children have gathered, read them the poem that you have chosen, and make reference to the bulletin board. (See Bulletin Board Ideas/Pets.) Discuss pets with the children. How many in the group have pets? What kinds of pets do they have? (Use this information to make one or more graphs. See Supplementary Activities/Graphing.) Invite the children to make, and/or to bring in, pet pictures to put onto the bulletin board.

3. Pet Names: Think of some common pet names that you have heard, place them on banners and streamers, and hang them about the room. Include some of the names of pets from books with which the children might be familiar. *(Harry, Clifford, Pinkerton, Clyde, Snoopy, etc.)*

   If you have a pet, use your pet's name, and make up a limerick about it. If not, you may wish to use the name of the dog in the story, Genevieve. (Rhyme pattern of a limerick is aabba.) Print out the limerick, and have that in the area where the children will gather.

   For example: There once was a dog, Genevieve,
                     Who from murky waters did retrieve,
                     No, not a ball, a bone, or such
                     For things like that don't matter much,
                     A girl, who was truly relieved.

   After the children come together, ask for volunteers to read the names on the streamers. Read the limerick to the children. Discuss the names of pets, and how they happened to be given the names that they have.

   Ask volunteers to make illustrations of their pets and to write explanations about why the pets were named as they are. Put these on the bulletin board. (See Bulletin Board Ideas/Pet Names.)

Bulletin Board Ideas

1. France: Make the entire bulletin board into a replica of the flag of France. Divide the bulletin board into three equal vertical sections. Cover the left vertical section with blue paper, the middle vertical section with white paper, and the right vertical section with red paper.

2. Pets: Cover the bulletin board with background paper. If you have or have had a pet, put some pictures of your pet on the bulletin board. If you do not have a pet, find some pictures in magazines of people with their pets, and place a few of those on the bulletin board. These will be taken down when the children make or bring pictures of their pets to share and these are put onto the board.

   You may decide that you really like some of the poems that you have located about different pets, and may wish to add one of those to the display, too.

3. Pet Names: Cover the bulletin board with background paper. Make a caption for it, such as: "What's In A Name?" Display the illustrations and explanations of pet names made by the children. (See Introductory Activity/Pet Names, above.)

Introduce the Story

Show the children the picture on the cover of the book. Have a volunteer read the title. Make predictions about what the story will be about. Record the predictions. Check them after the story has been read.

Has anyone in the group heard a story about the girl Madeline? What do you know about her? In what country does she live? As the story is read, look carefully at the illustrations. Ludwig Bemelmans, the author and illustrator of the book, fills the outdoor scenes with details of Paris.

Note: Selections from this guide may be used with the book Madeline *if you wish to introduce the character to the children before using* Madeline's Rescue. *The French theme of the Introductory Activity and the bulletin board, as well as some of the Supplementary Activities could easily be adapted for use.*

Procedure

It is suggested that this story be read in its entirety, if it is read to the group, and that you stop at some time during the reading to make some predictions. If it is to be read by the children, you may wish to utilize the DRTA Procedure, Directed Reading Thinking Activity, reading one section at a time. The questions and activities are given for the DRTA procedure. If you choose to read the story in its entirety, please read over the questions and activities, and make choices from them.

Before reading, you may wish to have the children demonstrate prior knowledge of some of the words. Have them share what they think the words mean and record their simple definitions. After reading, verify the meaning of each word with the children.

Using Predictions in the Novel Unit Approach

We all make predictions as we read—little guesses about what will happen next, how a conflict will be resolved, which details will be important to the plot, which details will help fill in our sense of a character. Students should be encouraged to predict, to make sensible guesses as they read the novel.

As students work on their predictions, these discussion questions can be used to guide them: What are some of the ways to predict? What is the process of a sophisticated reader's thinking and predicting? What clues does an author give to help us make predictions? Why are some predictions more likely to be accurate than others?

Create a chart for recording predictions. This could be either an individual or class activity. As each subsequent chapter is discussed, students can review and correct their previous predictions about plot and characters as necessary.

Use the facts and ideas the author gives.

Use your own prior knowledge.

Apply any new information (i.e., from class discussion) that may cause you to change your mind.

Predictions:

_____

_____

_____

_____

Prediction Chart

What characters have we met so far?	What is the conflict in the story?	What are your predictions?	Why did you make those predictions?

Story Map

Characters_____

_____

```
   ╭─────────╮
  (  Setting  )
   ╰─────────╯
        │
        ▼
   ╭─────────╮
  (  Problem  )
   ╰─────────╯
        │
        ▼
   ╭─────────╮
  (   Goal    )
   ╰─────────╯
        │
        ▼
   ╭─────────╮
  (  Episodes )
   ╰─────────╯
        │
        ▼
   ╭─────────╮
  ( Resolution )
   ╰─────────╯
```

Time and Place_____

_____

Problem_____

_____

_____

Goal_____

_____

_____

Beginning ──────▶ Development ──────▶ Outcome

_____

_____

_____

_____

_____

Resolution_____

_____

_____

_____

Using Character Webs in the Novel Unit Approach

Attribute webs are simply a visual representation of a character from the novel. They provide a systematic way for students to organize and recap the information they have about a particular character. Attribute webs may be used after reading the novel to recapitulate information about a particular character, or completed gradually as information unfolds. They may be completed individually or as a group project.

One type of character attribute web uses these divisions:

- How a character acts and feels. (How does the character act? How do you think the character feels? How would you feel if this happened to you?)

- How a character looks. (Close your eyes and picture the character. Describe him/her to me.)

- Where a character lives. (Where and when does the character live?)

- How others feel about the character. (How does another specific character feel about our character?)

In group discussion about the characters described in student attribute webs, the teacher can ask for backup proof from the novel. Inferential thinking can be included in the discussion.

Attribute webs need not be confined to characters. They may also be used to organize information about a concept, object, or place.

Attribute Web

The attribute web below will help you gather clues the author provides about a character in the novel. Fill in the blanks with words and phrases which tell how the character acts and looks, as well as what the character says and what others say about him or her.

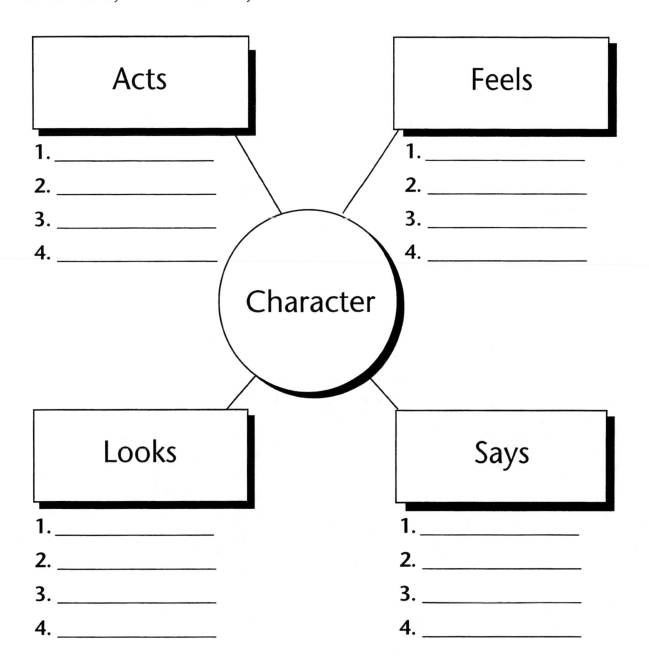

Acts

1. _____
2. _____
3. _____
4. _____

Feels

1. _____
2. _____
3. _____
4. _____

Character

Looks

1. _____
2. _____
3. _____
4. _____

Says

1. _____
2. _____
3. _____
4. _____

Attribute Web

© Novel Units, Inc.

12

The pages in this book are unnumbered. Numbers have been assigned to pages, starting with number 1 as the story begins.

Pages 1 through 11 (From "In an old house in Paris..." to " 'Good night, good night, dear Miss Clavel!' ")

Vocabulary

twelve (1)   straight (1)   camomile (10)

Vocabulary Activity

Camomile/chamomile: An aromatic plant native to Eurasia, having finely dissected leaves and white flowers. Eurasia: The continents of Europe and Asia and their offshore islands.

Discuss camomile, (chamomile), tea with the group. Has anyone in the group ever had it? In what other story was a character given camomile tea because he was not feeling well? *(In the story of Peter Rabbit, Peter was given camomile tea by his mother.)* Does someone in your family give you something warm to drink when you are not feeling well? If so, what is it? If possible, make some camomile tea and allow the children to taste it.

Discussion Questions and Activities
1. Where does the story take place? *(Page 1, The story takes place in Paris.)*
2. Have a world map, as well as a map of France on display. Locate France on the world map, and Paris on the map of France. (See additional activities in the supplementary section.)
3. Tell us something about Madeline. *(Page 1, She is the smallest of the 12 girls, not afraid of mice or tigers, and loves winter, snow, and ice.)*
4. Why is it that Madeline falls into the water? *(Pages 2-3, Madeline is walking on the ledge on the side of the bridge. She slips, and falls into the water.)*
5. How is Madeline rescued? *(Pages 6-7, A dog jumps into the water, and drags Madeline to the embankment.)* Have you ever heard or read of a dog that has rescued a person from a dangerous situation? Tell us about it.
6. Look at the illustration of Miss Clavel and the girls helping Madeline and the dog. *(page 9)* What are some of the the things that they are doing? Can you think of anything else that they could do to be helpful?
7. Does Miss Clavel scold Madeline? Do you think that Madeline has learned her lesson, and will no longer walk on the ledge of the bridge? Why do you think as you do?
8. Where is the dog as Miss Clavel bids the girls good night? *(See illustration on page 11.)*
9. Look at the faces of the girls as they lie in bed. Why do you think only one of them is happy? *(page 11)*
10. Start a character attribute web for Miss Clavel. Add to it as the story evolves. (See pages 10-12 of this guide.)
11. Start a story map. Many stories have the same parts: a setting, a problem, characters, a goal, and a series of events that lead to an ending or resolution of the problem. These elements may be placed on a story map. Just as a road map leads a driver from one place to another, a story map leads a reader from one point to another. (See page 9 of this guide.)
12. Make a prediction. What do you think will happen next? (See pages 7-8 of this guide.)

Pages 12 through 23 (From "Miss Clavel turned out the light." to " 'Go away and don't come back!' ")

Vocabulary

fight (12)	clever (13)	biscuits (14)
quickly (16)	annual (18)	children (21)
scat (23)		

Vocabulary Activities

1. Ask for a volunteer to define the word *scat*. When do you think that word would be used? What are some different words that could be used instead? *(Scat: To go away hastily; leave at once. Usually used in the imperative.)*
2. What are some words that rhyme with the word *scat*? Make a list. *(cat, rat, bat, fat, hat, mat, pat, sat, vat, flat, splat, etc.)*
3. Does anyone know what the word *annual* means? *(Annual: Recurring; done or performed every year; yearly. Botany: Living and growing for only one year or season.)* Do you know of anything that is done annually? *(parade, show, etc.)* Make a list.

Discussion Questions and Activities

1. What happens after Miss Clavel turns out the light? *(Page 12, The girls have a fight over where the dog will sleep that night.)* We are not told by the author about the outcome of the fight. What do you think happened?
2. Look at the illustration on page 13. It shows the dog in class. It makes a word with some letter-blocks. Look at the letters on all of the blocks. Print them out on a large sheet of paper, or on the chalkboard. *(C A T Y Q R G Z O H X P F L B)* What additional words would you be able to make with the letters on the blocks? *(Here are a few of them: bat, rat, pat, flat, flab, cot, pot, hot, got, bay, ray, gay, pay, play, clay, etc.)*
3. What name is the dog given? *(Page 14, Genevieve)* Do you like the name? What name would you give to the dog? Why?
4. How long has the dog been with the girls by the first of May? *(Page 16, The dog has been there six months.)*
5. What happens on the first of May? *(Page 18, The trustees come for the annual inspection.)* Why do you think the trustees make an inspection? What do you think they do? What would you look for if you were a trustee? *(Trustee: A person or agency that makes important decisions about how a school is run and how money is spent.)*
6. What happens when Genevieve is found by the trustees? *(Pages 20-23, Genevieve is de-bowed and put out of the door.)* How are the girls feeling? How is Genevieve feeling? Would you feel the same way? Draw a picture of you, showing how you would feel.
7. Does Miss Clavel want Genevieve to leave? *(Page 21, No. She asks that Genevieve be allowed to stay because the children love her.)*
8. What do you think will happen next? Make some predictions.
9. Write a class letter to the trustees, giving reasons as to why Genevieve should be allowed to stay.

Pages 24 through 33 (From "Madeline jumped on a chair." to " 'Genevieve, please come back to me.' "

Vocabulary
might (28)   believe (32)

Vocabulary Activities
1. Think of as many words that you can which rhyme with the word might. Make a list. *(bright, flight, slight, sight, blight, light, delight, fight, height, night, tight, right, etc.)*
2. Put the two words on a large sheet of paper, or on the chalkboard. Ask for volunteers to use both of the words in the same sentence. Record each sentence as it is given. Underline the vocabulary words.

Discussion Questions and Activities
1. After Genevieve is put out, what is it that Madeline proposes they do? *(Pages 24-25, Madeline suggests that they go out to look for Genevieve.)* How does Miss Clavel feel? *(Look at the illustration on page 25. She is crying.)*
2. Look at the illustrations on pages 26 through 32. Where are the girls looking for Genevieve? Do they find her? *(No)*
3. If you were looking for a lost dog in your community, where would you go to look?
4. What other things do people often do when a pet is lost? *(Put up signs in the neighborhood, ask neighbors, put ads in the paper, etc.)*
5. Where do you think that Genevieve has gone?
6. Make some predictions. Will Genevieve return to the girls?
7. Continue the story map as well as the attribute web for Miss Clavel.
8. Pretend that you are the girls. Make some posters about Genevieve to place in the neighborhood.

Pages 34 through 46 (From "In the middle of the night..." to "To go all around.")

Vocabulary
second (39)

Vocabulary Activity
Find all of the "second" things that you can in the room. The second light, the second tile, the second child, the second desk, the second table, etc. What is it that you have to know before you can find the second of anything? *(What it is that you are declaring to be the first! You must know what is first before you can designate what it is that is second.)*

Discussion Questions and Activities
1. Does Genevieve return to the girls? When? *(Pages 34-35, Miss Clavel hears Genevieve at the door in the middle of the night.)*
2. Where do the girls take Genevieve first? *(Page 36, to the kitchen where they pet and feed her.)*

3. Look at the illustration on page 37. The girls are in bed. Look at their faces. What happened before in the story when they looked like that? *(They had a fight about where Genevieve would sleep.)* Do you think that the same thing will happen again?

4. What does Miss Clavel declare when she finds that the girls are fighting about Genevieve? *(Page 41, Miss Clavel tells the girls that if there is one more fight, Genevieve will have to leave!)*

5. Look at Genevieve's face in the illustration on page 41. Do you think that she understands what Miss Clavel is saying? (Can pets tell by the tone of the voice, and the manner in which things are said just how a person is feeling?) Discuss. Say something in an angry way, a happy way, etc. Do people also know how someone else is feeling by the tone of voice used, and the manner in which something is said?

6. Why does one of the girls awaken Miss Clavel for the third time that night? *(Page 45, Genevieve has 12 puppies!)*

7. Page 46 has an illustration showing the girls going for a walk with Miss Clavel, each girl having her own puppy. Genevieve is leading the way. Where do you think that Genevieve sleeps at night?

8. Complete the story map as well as the attribute web for Miss Clavel.

9. How does the ending of the story make you feel? Would you change it in any way? If so, how?

Supplementary Activities

1. Madeline's Name: Madeline's name begins with the letter/sound of M. Make lists of all of the girl's and boy's names that can be thought of that begin with that same letter/sound.
   For example:

Girl's Names Beginning With M	Boy's Names Beginning With M
Madeline	Malcolm
Mandy	Marcus
Marcia	Mark
Margaret	Martin
Marguerite	Matthew
Maria	Michael
Marie	Marvin
Marianne	Maurice
Martha	Melvin
Martina	Milton
Martine	Myron
Mary	Maxwell
Maureen	Murray
Maxine	Morgan
Megan	Mack
Melanie	
Melissa	
Melody	
Meredith	
Michaela	
Michelle	
Monica	

How many people in the class have names that begin with the letter/sound of **M**?

When telling how many, do so in comparison to the group total. For example: If two of the children in a group of 28 have names that begin with that letter/sound, say, "Two of the twenty-eight children in the group have names that begin with the letter/sound of **M**." Show the children how that may be recorded as 2/28.

2. Other **M** Words: Make a list of other words that begin with the letter/sound of **M**. How long will it be?

Display the list in an accessible place so that words may be added to the list at any time.

(If desired, the children may be divided into cooperative groups, and given a specific amount of time in which to generate a list of words that begin with the letter/sound of **M**. The lists may then be compared, and a class list made.)

Make up tongue twisters, using the words from all of the **M** lists. Start with short ones, and increase in length. Try to say the tongue twisters three times, going faster and faster as they become familiar.

For example:

Marvin's Mustache (Moustache)
Marvin's Marvelous Mustache
Marvin's Magnificent Marvelous Mustache
Marvin's Madly Magnificent Marvelous Mustache
Marvin's Magical Madly Magnificent Marvelous Mustache

Macaroni Machine
Muddy Macaroni Machine
Mad Muddy Macaroni Machine
Marvelous Mad Muddy Macaroni Machine
Mark's Marvelous Mad Muddy Macaroni Machine

3. Other Names: Names of imaginary people may be invented. Have some fun, and make up some names. Using initials is helpful. Make illustrations to go with them.
For example:

Dan D. Lion	I. C. Cream	C. U. Soon
Sugar N. Spice	U. R. Nice	T. Bag
Salt N. Pepper	Don Key	R. E. Bock
I. C. You	I. L. B. Wright	T. Cup

4. Story Poem: Ludwig Bemelmans wrote the story of *Madeline's Rescue* in rhyme. Make up a group poem that tells a story. (Add on adventures to the following, if you like, as a start.)

Jean	Sam
On a tree-lined street,	Out in the wood
Oh, serene,	By the #1 dam
Lived a little girl	Roamed a boy
By the name of Jean.	By the name of Sam.
She walked her dog	He stopped often
To and fro,	On his way,
For far from home	For there was no hurry
She did not go.	On that fine sunny day.
Often there was	He smelled the flowers,
By her side	And felt the moss.
A big white duck.	Dipped his toes in the water
It was very wide.	And on rocks did cross.
Joining in the walk,	From side to side,
You see,	Over ripple and such.
From fence post	He was thought very brave,
To maple tree.	But it didn't take much.
At the end of the walk	Sam saw a chipmunk,
Those same three	And then a mouse.
Would swing on	Each little creature
That maple tree.	Ran to its own house.
What a sight	Sam looked and inspected
It was to view	Each thing that he could,
On that swing.	Leaving each alone
A girl, a dog, and a wide duck, too!	In its place in the wood.

5. What If?: One change in circumstance may change the outcome of a situation. Consider the following, and/or make up some of your own. Tell about the outcome of each situation.

What if Genevieve had not been near the bridge?

What if Miss Clavel had not allowed Genevieve to stay with the girls?

What if Genevieve had not returned after she was turned out of the house by the trustees?

What if Genevieve had not had puppies?

6. Write A Letter: Imagine that you are corresponding with a child living in France. Tell that child something about yourself.

Think about the questions that you want to ask about France. Do not overwhelm your correspondent. Ask only three questions. What will they be?

If you would really like a pen pal from France, write to these people, being sure to tell them that the location is France:

International Pen Friends
P.O. Box 290065
Brooklyn, NY 11229

Worldwide Pen Friends
P.O. Box 6896
Thousand Oaks, CA 91359

7. Guests: Invite guests into the classroom, to tell the children about France, or to teach them a bit of the language. The well from which to draw may include exchange students, foreign language teachers, senior citizen travelers, and military personnel.

Before your guest(s) arrive, have a group discussion regarding the kinds of information that you will be listening for, and the questions that might be asked if something specific has not been mentioned that the group would really like to know. (Arrangements with guests should be made beforehand, so that each knows the purpose of the visit, and what is expected.) Readiness on the part of the children, attentive behavior, and appreciation of each guest's contribution is the price paid for the "ticket to France."

8. Graphing: Use large butcher or craft paper. Make a large grid on the paper. Make a thick baseline on the graph, and record the kinds of pets that were discussed in the Introductory Activity. Also have a space for "none."

Give each child a piece of paper that will fit into a grid box. Students are to record their own name on the paper, and attach the paper to the graph, using a gluestick. Remind the children to start at the baseline, and to move up from there.

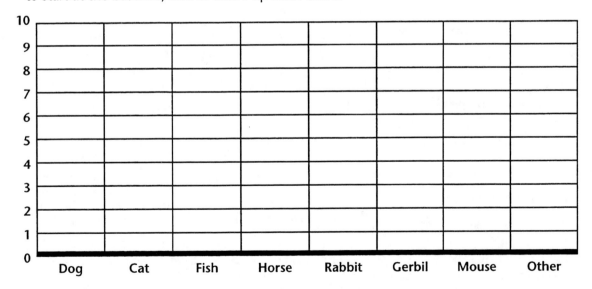

Make some concluding statements about the graph. What has the most? the least? How many more _____ than _____? How many children do not have pets? Are there more children with or without pets?

You may also wish to make an additional graph from these suggestions: color of pets, size of pets, pet housing.

9. Metric: The metric system of measurement is used in France. (See Teacher Information.)

The meter is the basic unit of measurement. Cut some pieces of string into one meter lengths. Have children in partners measure things in the room with the string. Can you find three things that are about a meter long? Compare with others. How many meters long is the room? the hallway? etc.

The meter is the unit of measure for many races in Olympic track meets. With the cooperation of the physical education instructor, arrange to have a 50-meter dash.

Pretend that a paper plate is a discus. How many meters can you throw it? Mark off an area, such as a hall, in meter lengths, and find out. Use the same area to find out how far you can throw a javelin, using a paper straw. Keep a record of your results. Can you improve with practice?

10. Cooking Metric: To cook metric, you will need a dry measuring set marked in milliliters, and a set of metric measuring spoons. You will also need a clear measure marked in milliliters for measuring liquids. Check out the science equipment. You may find just what you need right there.

Chocolate Chip Cookies

Preheat oven to 350° F. (180° C)

In a mixing bowl, stir together thoroughly, using a wooden spoon:

250 ml margarine	or	220 g margarine
175 ml light brown sugar	or	150 g light brown sugar
175 ml granulated sugar	or	150 g granulated sugar

Add and stir well:

    5 ml vanilla
    2 eggs

Mix together:

550 ml flour	or	500 g flour
5 ml baking soda		
2 ml salt		

Add gradually to other ingredients and mix well.

Add and stir into cookie mixture:

    1 package chocolate chips (170 g)

Drop by teaspoonful (about 15 ml) onto ungreased cookie sheet. Leave space of about 4 cm between the cookies so that they won't run into each other when they bake. You can put two cookie sheets into the oven to bake at one time. Bake 8 to 10 minutes. Remove the cookies from the cookie sheet with a pancake turner. Before putting another batch of cookies on the sheet, scrape off any bits of cookie crumbs, and wipe the cookie sheet with a paper towel. Makes about 96 cookies.

11. Twelve: There are twelve girls living in the house in Paris with Miss Clavel. Let's find out some things about twelve.

    Give each child a set of twelve objects, such as beans, bottle caps, chips, etc.

    (To the teacher: Do this on successive days, allowing plenty of time each day for the discovering of combinations.)

    Ask the children to arrange the twelve objects into two sets. What can each child find out about the sets he/she has made? Make a record of the discoveries. Display.

    Have the twelve objects arranged into three sets, and continue the process.

    Have the twelve objects arranged into four sets, and continue the process.

12. Maps: Using the world map, find out the distance between Paris, France and your location.

    Discuss how you would get to Paris from your location.

    Looking at the map of France, note distances from Paris, and compare. (For example: Is it farther from Paris to Lyon or from Paris to Bordeaux?) You may even want to use lengths of string to compare the distances on the map.

13. Are You Sleeping?: Print out the French words to this familiar song. Teach the French version to the children, or request that one of your guests do so. Run your hand under the French words as the song is sung. Sing the song in rounds.

    > *Frère Jacques*
    > *Frère Jacques*
    >
    > *Dormez vous,*
    > *Dormez vous.*
    >
    > *Sonnez les matines,*
    > *Sonnez les matines,*
    >
    > *Ding! Dang! Dong!*
    > *Ding! Dang! Dong!*

    The Great Rounds Songbook, (See Bibliography/Nelson), has two additional rounds from France, "French Cathedrals," and "Vent Frais/Cool Wind."

14. Art: Bring in whatever is available to share the art of France with the children. Perhaps your library has prints for you to check out. The local high school may have some for you to borrow from the foreign language department or the art department.

    Check out books from the library that have pictures of the art and artists of France. Share information about the lives of these artists, as well as enjoy the works of art.

15. Music and Poetry: French musicians and poets have contributed much to our world. It would not be possible to include here the many who have done so. It is suggested that you get reference material from your local library. I have included in the bibliography two resources that I have found very valuable. (Applebaum and Hemming on page 31 of this guide.)

Culminating Activity

Plan an imaginary trip to Paris! Enlist the help of a travel agent or an airline servicing France, and have a wonderful time! [Air France has an alliance with Delta: 0 802 802 802 (France) or 800/241-4141 (U.S.); TWA: 800/221-2000; American Airlines: 800/433-7300; Delta: 800/241-4141]

Have the children think of places to go and things to do.

How much money will it cost to go? Remember, you have to get to and from your location of departure. What other costs might you have? Where will you stay?

Explain the use of passports, and have each child make one. If possible, use a school picture, or a snapshot for the picture needed for the passport. (You may be fortunate enough to enlist the help of a passport photographer, too. Give it a try!)

You will need to know the weather conditions, so you will know what to pack. Make a suitcase out of paper, and make representations of the clothes and other items that you will need. Put them into the suitcase. Be prepared!

Average daily maximum and minimum temperatures for Paris:

January—	43°F	6°C	May—	68°F	20°C	September—	70°F	21°C
	34°F	1°C		49°F	10°C		53°F	12°C
February—	45°F	7°C	June—	73°F	23°C	October—	60°F	16°C
	34°F	1°C		55°F	10°C		46°F	8°C
March—	54°F	12°C	July—	76°F	24°C	November—	50°F	10°C
	39°F	4°C		58°F	14°C		40°F	5°C
April—	60°F	16°C	August—	75°F	24°C	December—	44°F	7°C
	43°F	6°C		58°F	14°C		36°F	2°C

Visit a local bakery, and purchase some French bread to take back to the classroom to eat.

Prepare some food in the French way to taste and enjoy. (See Recipe section for some suggestions.)

Make some postcards to "send" to friends and family. What will you tell them about your trip?

Keep a diary of your adventure. What did you think about your trip to Paris?

Crossword Puzzle

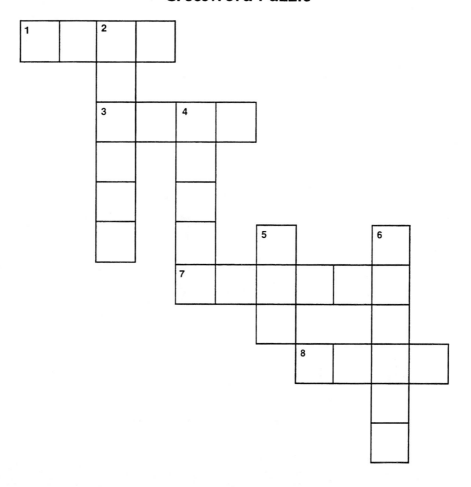

(Words used in this puzzle: second, riot, tea, twelve, night, nine, annual, year.)

Across
1. Twelve months
3. Number after eight
7. Number after eleven
8. Outbreak

Down
2. Yearly
4. Opposite of day
5. Beverage
6. After first

Vocabulary Word Search

Do the puzzles. For something extra to do, copy the letters that have not been used in the order given, from the top to the bottom of the puzzle, going from left to right on each line. Keep the letters in order.

Group the letters into words to make a sentence.

n	i	g	h	t	f	t	b	l
a	i	h	o	p	e	h	a	i
m	e	n	f	d	d	l	c	n
e	o	y	e	a	r	o	k	e
g	m	i	l	k	i	v	g	s
s	w	a	l	k	o	e	t	a
s	l	e	e	p	t	y	e	d

LINES   DOG
SLEEP   FELL
LOVE   HOPE
FED   YEAR
NIGHT   BACK
MILK   NINE
WALK   RIOT
NAME

(Answer: THE DOG STAYED)

Vocabulary Word Search

Do the puzzles. For something extra to do, copy the letters that have not been used in the order given, from the top to the bottom of the puzzle, going from left to right on each line. Keep the letters in order.

Group the letters into words to make a sentence.

t	w	e	l	v	e	m	a	b	q	c	d
c	e	s	e	c	o	n	d	i	u	l	e
h	n	a	r	o	u	n	d	s	i	e	l
i	o	i	n	n	e	s	l	c	c	v	i
l	u	p	p	n	e	d	o	u	k	e	m
d	g	n	t	h	u	n	t	i	l	r	i
r	h	e	b	s	c	a	t	t	y	r	g
e	f	i	g	h	t	i	l	s	d	g	h
n	s	m	a	l	l	e	s	t	e	x	t

TWELVE	QUICKLY
UNTIL	SCAT
FIGHT	ANNUAL
BISCUITS	MIGHT
CHILDREN	SECOND
SMALLEST	ENOUGH
TEA	AROUND
CLEVER	

(Answer: MADELINE SLIPPED ON THE BRIDGE.)

Legend
X = Period (.)

Teacher Information

France

Capital:	Paris
Official Language:	French
Government:	Democratic Republic, having a president, a prime minister, and a parliament form as its present government.
Flag:	The flag is called the "tricolor," and is divided into equal red, white, and blue vertical stripes. The three colors were first used as a French emblem on July 17, 1789, during the French Revolution.
National Song:	*"La Marseillaise"*
National Motto:	*Liberté, Egalité, Fraternité* (Liberty, Equality, Fraternity)
Money:	The franc is the standard monetary unit.
Weights and Measures:	France uses the metric system.
Occupations:	Services, 64 percent; industry, 32 percent; agriculture, 4 percent
Borders:	Italy, Spain, Switzerland, Germany, Belgium, and Luxembourg

The French people love their children, and love being around them. However, parents expect children to be well behaved and courteous. It is rare to see a French child yell or scream in public.

French children seem to be aware that their parents work very hard, so they usually help out around home. Some children do the grocery shopping at small neighborhood stores, others may set the table or even start dinner, especially if both parents work. Most French children like to spend time with their grandparents. In some families, the parents, children, and grandparents live in the same house. More often, the grandparents live close by.

Schooling in France begins early in life, and is quite demanding. Most children attend nursery schools or kindergartens. They may start as young as two years of age, although compulsory elementary education does not begin in France until the age of six.

French children must go to school from the ages of six to sixteen. At the age of six, they go to primary schools. When they are eleven years of age, they go to secondary schools. The Ministry of National Education decides what subjects are to be taught in the secondary schools, and what teaching methods will be used. The schools do not usually have choirs, clubs, bands, or sports programs of their own. The Secretary of State for Youth and Sports organizes these activities for Wednesday afternoon, when the schools are closed. To make up for this closure on Wednesday, the children go to school on Saturday morning.

On regular school days, classes usually begin at 9:00 am and continue until 4:30 pm, with an hour and a half off for lunch. There are also two hours of homework each night. Discipline is strict, and the children have great respect for their teachers.

When children are sixteen they may leave school or stay on for one to three years, taking courses to prepare them for their chosen work or for national diplomas. The examination to enter a university is very difficult, and up to 35 percent of the candidates fail it. The French equivalent of a doctoral degree is one of the most difficult in the world to obtain.

Delicious foods are part of every French meal. At breakfast, people often eat tasty croissants. They may also enjoy slices of *la baguette*, a long loaf of sourdough bread, covered with butter and jam. At lunch the meal will include tasty meats and vegetables, a salad, and a sweet dessert. Except in the largest cities, the lunch break lasts about two hours. Even the stores close up. After the meal is finished, people talk, read, or go for a walk. Pastries may be eaten anytime, but they are most often enjoyed at *les quatre heures*, four o'clocks, which is the French tea time or snack time. A hot cocoa or *café au lait* would be served with the sweets. A late, light dinner may consist of soup and cold meats with fruit, yogurt, or cheese for dessert.

Many French people have been important in modern science and engineering. Among them are Antoine Laurent Lavoisier, known as the father of modern chemistry; Marie and Pierre Curie, discoverers of the chemical element radium; André Ampère, founder of the science of electro-dynamics/electromagnetism; and Louis Pasteur, whose work led to the germ theory of disease.

Literature, the theater, painting, and films play an important part in French culture. The arts have a long tradition of brilliant writers, playwrights, and painters, of whom the French are justly proud. Famous writers are known throughout every age, and include Diderot, Voltaire, Montesquieu, Rousseau, de Balzac, Dumas, Proust, Victor Hugo, Sartre, and Camus, the latter having received the Nobel Prize for Literature in 1957.

Famous playwrights include Molière, Corneille, Racine, Anouilh, Giraudoux, Genet, and Ionesco. Influential French painters include de la Tour, Poussin, Watteau, David, Manet, Monet, Corot, Pissarro, Renoir, Seurat, Degas, Toulouse-Laútrec, Gauguin, Matisse, Cézanne, Braque, and Van Gogh.

Film-making is held in such esteem in France that it is known as "the Seventh Art." One of the earliest films, presented in 1895, was made by two French brothers, the Lumières. Jean Renoir, the son of the painter Auguste Renoir and born in 1894, was considered one of the greatest early film-makers. Later directors included Truffaut, Godard, Chabrol, Malle, and Deville.

Sports are a growing part of French life. There are over 60 different sports associations in France, and over 100,000 sports clubs. The most popular sport is soccer. The world's most famous cycling race is the Tour de France, first held in 1903. Over 3,000 miles of arduous terrain is covered by the cyclists. Tennis, skiing, fencing, and rugby football are also very popular.

Find out more about France.

Some French words used in English

café	cliché	cul-de-sac
restaurant	hors d'oeuvres	chef
entrée	paté	menu
quiche	eclair	croissant
buffet	nougat	mousse
berét	soufflé	role
discothèque	crochet	chic
boutique	fiancé/fiancée	rendezvous

Counting in French

1	*un*	11	*onze*
2	*deux*	12	*douze*
3	*trois*	13	*treize*
4	*quatre*	14	*quatorze*
5	*cinq*	15	*quinze*
6	*six*	16	*seize*
7	*sept*	17	*dix sept*
8	*huit*	18	*dix huit*
9	*neuf*	19	*dix neuf*
10	*dix*	20	*vingt*

Months of the Year

janvier	January
février	February
mars	March
avril	April
mai	May
juin	June
juillet	July
août	August
septembre	September
octobre	October
novembre	November
décembre	December

Days of the Week

lundi	Monday
mardi	Tuesday
mercredi	Wednesday
jeudi	Thursday
vendredi	Friday
samedi	Saturday
dimanche	Sunday

Seasons of the Year

l'été	summer
le printemps	spring
l'hiver	winter
l'automne	fall

The Metric System

The word metric comes from the Greek word *metron,* meaning measure. It is a system of measurement based on mathematics. The metric system began with the French, in 1790. After the French Revolution, the new government wanted a different way of doing almost everything. The Paris Academy of Sciences was asked to construct a new system of weights and measures based on the best scientific knowledge of the time. Scientists, including Pierre Simon Laplace and Antoine Laurent Lavoisier, decided to make the standard of length a portion of the Earth's surface. The portion used was the distance form the North Pole to the Equator, which is a quarter of the distance around the Earth and called a quadrant. The quadrant was divided into 10 million equal parts, and each of these parts was called a meter. All other units of length were based on the meter.

The scientists also decided to use the decimal system as a base, so that all units would be based on 10. The French developed a similar system for weight and volume, and by 1795 laws had been passed requiring everyone in France to use the metric way of measurement. However, the people were slow to change their ways and it was not until 1837 that another law was passed making the metric system the only system to be used in France after January 1, 1840.

Recipes
Crêpes

1 cup all-purpose flour
¼ teaspoon baking powder
1¼ cups milk
1 egg
1 teaspoon margarine or butter, melted

Mix flour and baking powder in medium-sized bowl. Stir in other ingredients. Beat entire mixture by hand, or with beater, until smooth. Lightly butter medium-sized skillet. Heat skillet at moderate temperature until butter bubbles.

Pour ¼ cup of the batter into skillet. Immediately turn skillet from side to side so that batter covers bottom in a thin film. Cook batter until small bubbles begin to form on top of the crêpe. Run a wide spatula underneath edges of crêpe to loosen it. Flip the crêpe over and cook other side until it turns a golden color. Remove crêpe from skillet. Stack cooked crêpes on plate and serve warm. (Serves 6)

Serving suggestion: Set out small custard dishes filled with jellies, jams, fresh fruit slices, whipped cream or topping. Put a topping on the crêpe and roll it up.

Croque Monsieur

1 slice bread, toasted
1 slice Swiss cheese
1 slice ham
butter or margarine

Spread butter or margarine on bread. Put on ham and cheese. Place this open-faced sandwich in oven and heat at 425° F for about 10 minutes. Remove and serve.

Three Cheese Quiche

1¾ cups flour, sifted
1 stick salted butter or margarine
7 tablespoons ice water
¼ pound small curd cottage cheese
2 tablespoons milk
6 medium-sized mushrooms, sliced (optional)
½ cup grated Swiss cheese
¼ wheel bonbel-type cheese, cubed
2 eggs, beaten

Sift flour into medium-sized bowl. Cut up butter into seven or eight pieces. Make a hollow space in center of flour and add pieces of butter. Using a pastry blender or your fingers, mix butter and flour into granular dough. Make another hollow space in center of grainy dough mixture. Add 7 tablespoons of ice water. Mix until water is absorbed into dough. If dough will not hold together, add 1 or 2 more tablespoons of ice water. Form dough into ball. Cover it with a damp paper towel and refrigerate for 1 hour.

Preheat oven to 400° F.

Roll out pastry dough to about ¼ inch thickness on lightly floured surface. Line a 9- or 10-inch pie pan with dough. Lightly pierce entire bottom of this pastry shell with a fork to prevent dough from puffing up. Bake shell for 10 minutes. Remove from oven and allow to cool.

Combine cottage cheese, milk, Swiss cheese, bonbel cheese, eggs, and mushrooms, (if desired), in a medium-sized bowl. Pour cheese mixture into pastry shell.

Put shell back in oven and bake until filling turns golden color and shell light brown, about 30 to 45 minutes. Remove from oven, and allow quiche to cool slightly before cutting into pieces.

Salade D'épinards aux Lardons et au Vinaigre
(Spinach Salad With Bacon and Vinegar)

1 pound fresh spinach
2 hard-boiled eggs
¼ pound piece of bacon
3 tablespoons vinegar
salt and pepper

Discard spinach stems and wash leaves thoroughly. Drain them and pat dry with paper. Put them in a salad bowl. Separate egg whites from yolks. Coarsely chop whites and reserve; sieve yolks over the spinach.

Cut bacon into small cubes and sauté in a frying pan until crisp.

Discard all but about four tablespoons fat. Pour fat with bacon over spinach and toss immediately, the heat will wilt the leaves slightly. Add vinegar to frying pan and heat gently, stirring to dissolve pan juices. Pour over salad and toss again. Add pepper, toss thoroughly, and taste for seasoning, as salt may not be needed.

Sprinkle salad with chopped egg white and serve at once from the salad bowl.

Omelette
(Flat Omelet)

1 tablespoon butter
salt and pepper
1 tablespoon chopped parsley
4-5 eggs

In a medium bowl, whisk eggs with salt and pepper just until thoroughly mixed. Heat butter in a 9-inch omelet pan over medium heat until it stops sputtering and begins to brown. At once add egg mixture. Stir eggs briskly with flat of a fork and when eggs start to thicken continue stirring until mixture is as thick as scrambled eggs.

Leave omelet to cook 20-25 seconds, or until it is well-browned on the bottom and almost firm on top. Either flip the omelet with a spatula or take the pan from the heat, set on heatproof plate on top, and turn omelet onto it; slide omelet back into the pan and brown other side.
Serve hot or cold, cut in wedges.

Bibliography

Adler, Peggy. *Metric Puzzles.* NY: Watts, 1977.

Amery, Heather and Katherine Folliot. *The First Thousand Woods In French.* London: Usborne Publishing, Ltd., 1979.

Applebaum, Stanley, editor. *Introduction to French Poetry. A Dual Language Book.* NY: Dover Books, 1969.

Bender, Lionel. *France.* Morristown, NJ: Silver Burdett Press, 1988.

Bitter, Gary. *Exploring With Metrics.* NY: J. Messner, 1975.

Consolo, Paula, ed. *Fedor's 93.* NY: Fedor's Travel Publications, Inc.,1992.

Donovan, Frank. *Let's Go Metric.* NY: Weybright & Talley, 1974.

Gofen, Ethel. *France.* NY: Marshall Cavendish Corp., 1992.

Hazzen, Anne-Françoise. *Let's Learn French Coloring Book.* Lincolnwood, IL: Passport Books, 1990.

Hemming, Roy. *Discovering Music.* NY: Four Winds Press, 1974.

Holbrook, Sabra. *Growing Up In France.* NY: Atheneum, 1980.

Johnson, Anne, editor. *The Illustrated Escoffier: Recipes From The Classic French Tradition.* NY: International Culinary Society: Distributed by Crown Publishers, 1987.

McCleary, Julia. *Cooking Metric Is Fun.* NY: Harcourt Brace Jovanovich, 1979.

Mealer, Tamara. *My World In French/A Coloring Book and Picture Dictionary.* Lincolnwood, IL: Passport Books, 1992.

Morgenstern, Steven. *Metric Puzzles, Tricks, and Games.* NY: Sterling, 1978.

Nation, Kay. *Meters, Liters, and Grams: Understanding the Metric System.* NY: Hawthorne Books, 1975.

Nelson, Esther. *The Great Rounds Song Book.* NY: Sterling Publishing, 1985. Page 33 "Vent Frais/Cool Wind," Page 36 "French Cathedrals."

Norbrook, Dominique. *Passport To France.* NY: Watts, 1986.

Schur, Sylvia. *The Woman's Day New French Cookery.* Greenwich, CT: Fawcett Publications, 1977.

Tunnacliffe, Chantal. *France, the Land and Its People.* Morristown, NJ: Silver Burdett Press, 1986.

Waldee, Lynne. *Cooking the French Way.* Minneapolis, MN: Lerner Publications, 1982.

Willan, Anne. *Anne Willan's Basic French Cookery.* Tucson, AZ: H.P. Books, 1980.

Audio-Visual Bibliography

Bemelmans, Ludwig. *Madeline's Rescue.* (Sound Filmstrip) Weston, CT: Weston Woods Studios.

Chevalier, Maurice. *Movie Musicals, 1927-1936.* (Sound Recording/CD) London: BBC Records and Tapes, 1987. "What Would You Do?"

Debussy, Claude. *Boulez Conducts Debussy.* (Sound Recording/CD) NY: CBS Records, 1985.

Debussy, Claude. *Twentieth Century Composers/Arthur Fiedler.* (Sound Recording/Record) Alexandria, VA: Time-Life Records, 1981. "Reverie"

Debussy, Claude. *Amsterdam Guitar Trio Plays Music By Debussy, Faure, Chopin.* (Sound Recording/CD) NY: RCA Victor, 1988. "Suite Bergamasque," "Petite Suite"

Debussy, Claude. *Arabesque: Romantic Harp Music of the Nineteenth Century, Volume 2.* (Sound Recording/CD) London: Hyperion, 1984. "Arabesque No. 1," La Fille Aux Cheveux De Lin"

La Chanson Veveysane. *Christmas In France.* (Record/In French) New Rochelle, NY: Request Records, 1972.

Language School. *French For Children.* (Cassette/Book) Seattle, WA: The Language School, 1985.

Mahoney, Judy and Mary Cronan. *Teach Me French.* Minneapolis, MN: Teach Me Tapes, Inc., 1985.

Optimal Learning. *French For Tots.* (Cassette/Book) San Rafael, CA: Optimal Learning Language Land, 1988.

Piaf, Edith. *Edith Piaf.* (Sound Recording/ Cassette) Los Angeles, CA: LaserLight, 1990.

Piaf, Edith. *Edith Piaf At Carnegie Hall.* (Sound Recording/Record) NY: Peters International, 1977.

Spoken Arts. *French Songs For Children.* (Cassette/Book) New Rochelle, NY: Spoken Arts, 1975.

Audio-Visual and Print Sources

Request a catalog from

Rand McNally
P.O. Box 1697
Skokie, IL 60076

Dover Publications
31 East Second Street
Mineola, NY 11501

Music For Little People
Box 1460
Redway, CA 95560

For current information, maps, etc.

French Government Tourist Office
645 North Michigan Ave.
Chicago, IL 60611-2836

French Government Tourist Office
1981 McGill College Ave., Suite 490
Montreal, Quebec H3A 2W9

French Government Tourist Office
610 5th Ave.
New York, NY 10020

French Government Tourist Office
1 Dundas St. W, Suite 2405, Box 8
Toronto, Ontario M5G 1Z3

French Government Tourist Office
2305 Cedar Springs Rd.
Dallas, TX 75201

French Government Tourist Office
9401 Wilshire Blvd.
Beverly Hills, CA 90212

French Government Tourist Office
1 Hillidie Plaza, Suite 250
San Francisco, CA 94102

For a "Profile of France"

French Embassy Press and Information Service
4101 Reservoir Road, NW
Washington, DC 20007

Puzzle Answers

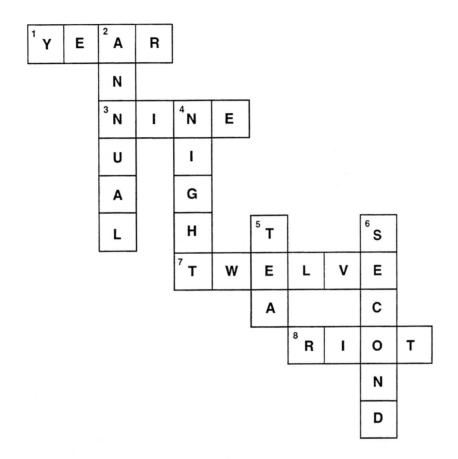

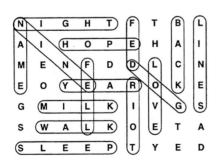

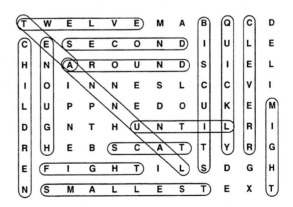

Notes

34

Notes

Notes